LIMITLESS

Life with Jesus

Limitless: Life with Jesus
ISBN: 978-0-9747558-4-7

Copyright © 2017 by Larry Hutton Ministries, Inc.
P.O. Box 822
Broken Arrow, OK 74013-0822
www.larryhutton.org

Published by Harrison House, LLC.
P.O. Box 35035
Tulsa, Oklahoma 74153
www.harrisonhouse.com

Welcome to the Family of God!

Whether you just received Jesus as Lord and Savior, or did so at an earlier time, you are part of an awesome family. There are many benefits, rights, and privileges that God has for His children, and they all belong to you!

As a child of God, regardless of your past, He has a wonderful future planned out for you, and it is filled with good things.

I am going to explain what actually took place when you received Jesus as your Savior. I will also briefly introduce to you some of the benefits that belong to you since you are now part of God's family.

This book will help you to understand what just happened to you, as well as provide more insight into what true Christianity is all about. The truths you are about to learn will help you to develop into a strong, stable Christian.

CHAPTER 1

The Problem

The first book of the Bible is Genesis. It tells us the story of creation. It also reveals that God created man to be just like Him.

Then, in the third chapter, we see the devil (Satan, Lucifer) persuade Adam and Eve to yield to temptation and succumb to sin. Their choice to disobey God and eat of the forbidden fruit caused them to die spiritually. To die spiritually means to be separated from God.

When Adam and Eve sinned they died on the inside. They were no longer connected to God. Without their knowledge Satan had become their God.

Herein lies the problem: Adam's name means mankind. When Adam sinned, death not only came upon *him*, it also passed on to *all humanity* that descended from him. Man's nature no longer had God's nature. He now had a fallen nature, a sinful one that was dead to (or separated from) God.

THAT AFFECTED YOU AND ME!

Because Adam was the father of humanity, his sin nature was transferred to the human race.

Romans 5:12 says, "Wherefore, as by one man sin entered into the world, and death by sin; and so *death passed upon all men*, for that all have sinned."

Notice, death passed to all men, which included you and me. Spiritual death (separation from God) is what causes mankind to have a sinful nature.

We were not sinners because of *our* sin. We were sinners because sin had been handed down to us from long ago.

As sinners, we were not in right standing with God. It is called "unrighteousness" in the Bible. No matter how hard we tried to please God, no matter how many good things we did, it did not make things "right" between us and God.

The Bible says that "no one is righteous and that all mankind has come up short of God's standard of dignity and honor" (Romans 3:10, 23 My Paraphrase).

This seems like a terrible dilemma. However, since God knows the future better then we know the past, He had already put a plan into place. This plan would give man the opportunity to come back to God—to transfer man from death back into life. Man would once again be "righteous" or, in right standing with his creator.

CHAPTER 2

The Answer

There are two questions that must be answered concerning a relationship with God.

1. How does man become right with God, even though he is a sinner and separated from Him?

2. Is there more than one way to become right with God?

Let me show you some Bible verses that answer both of these questions.

Romans 6:23

> **For the wages of sin is death; but the gift of God is eternal life through Jesus Christ our Lord.**

1st Corinthians 15:21–22

> **For since by man [Adam] came death, by Man [Jesus] also came**

the resurrection of the dead. ²²For as in Adam all die, even so in Christ all shall be made alive.

John 3:16

For God so loved the world that He gave His only begotten Son, that whoever believes in Him should not perish but have everlasting life.

John 14:6

I am the way, the truth, and the life. No one comes to the Father except by Me.

These Scriptures have answered our two questions. Let me restate them along with the answers.

1. How does man become right with God even though he is a sinner and separated from Him?

The answer: Jesus!

When we receive Jesus as our Lord and Savior, He raises us up from the dead and makes us alive unto God. He puts us back in right standing with God—making us righteous.

2. Is there more than one way to become right with God?

The answer: No. Jesus is the only way!

There are people who say that there are many ways to God. However, you can clearly see from the Scriptures we looked at, that their theory is not true. They are trying to figure out God's way with their human intellect.

The Bible says there is a way that seems right to man, but it leads to death. That is found in Proverbs 14:12 and 16:25.

God says there is only *one way* to Him, only *one way* to Heaven, and only *one way* to become part of the Kingdom of God. His name is Jesus. He is the *only way* for mankind to go from death (separation from God) back to life (brought back into right-standing with God).

The reason Jesus is the only way is because God put His life inside Jesus. This is revealed in 1st John 5:11–12.

And this is the record that God has given to us eternal life, and this life is in his Son. [12]He that has the Son has life; and he that has not the Son of God has not life.

Just think, you now have the life of God living on the inside of you!

As you learn to walk with Him you will discover that He is a loving, merciful, and good God.

God is not mad at you for the things you have done. In truth, He is not mad at any person for their sins.

This truth is found in the Bible in 2nd Corinthians 5:19.

It was God [personally present] in Christ, reconciling and restoring the world to favor with Himself, not counting up and holding against [men] their trespasses [but cancelling them], and committing to us the message of reconciliation (of the restoration to favor). (AMPC)

Wow! God has restored the world to favor with Himself! That includes you and me, but it also includes everyone else on the earth.

This verse shows us that God is not mad at humanity. He is not counting up or holding their sins against them. He has restored them to favor with Himself.

That is good news—which is one reason why the New Testament is called "Good News."

CHAPTER 3

Free From Sin

Now that you have received Jesus as your Lord and Savior, you are no longer separated from God. You have been forgiven of all your sins, and you have been given a position (or seat) in Heaven right next to Jesus.

The Apostle Paul, who wrote much of the New Testament, had some wonderful things to say about these very things in the book of Ephesians. Let us read them.

Ephesians 2:1, 4–6, 8–9

> Once you were dead because of your disobedience and your many sins. 4But God is so rich in mercy, and He loved us so much, 5that even though we were dead because of our sins, He gave us life when He raised Christ from the dead. (It is only by God's grace that you have

been saved!) ⁶For He raised us from the dead along with Christ and seated us with Him in the heavenly realms because we are united with Christ Jesus. ⁸*God saved you by His grace when you believed.* And you can't take credit for this; it is a gift from God. ⁹Salvation is not a reward for the good things we have done, so none of us can boast about it. (NLT)

Allow me to zero in on verses 8 and 9 for a moment. Verse 8 says you are saved by God's *grace*. Grace is the unmerited, undeserved, and unearned favor of God. Verses 8–9 say that *salvation is a gift*.

Salvation from God is a gift, not a purchase. It was given because of love (John 3:16), not because of something we did.

In other words, God did us a favor!

We did not purchase, earn, or deserve this gift of salvation. We simply believed in Jesus, and then God released His grace into our lives.

WHAT I AM ABOUT TO SAY
IS VITALLY IMPORTANT

We did not get *saved* based on what we did or did not do. Which means, we do not get *un-saved* by what we do or do not do!

God's salvation is not some shoddy way to become part of His family, only to be undone by our mistakes. His gift is much more durable and secure than that.

Titus 3:5 says, "He saved us because of his mercy, and not because of any good things that we have done. God washed us by the power of the Holy Spirit. He gave us new birth and a fresh beginning" (CEV).

When God saved us, He sent the Holy Spirit to live inside us. First Corinthians 3:16 informs us that we are the temple of God, and the Spirit of God lives in us.

When the Holy Spirit moved inside of us, He brought nine things along with Him. I liken them to nine pieces of baggage. In Galatians 5:22–23, they are called the "fruit of the Spirit."

Once the Holy Spirit takes up residence in us, He does not have to pack up His bags and leave every time we make a mistake. That would be a cheesy salvation package.

Look at Ephesians 1:13–14.

> **And you also became God's people when you heard the true message, the Good News that brought you salvation. You believed in Christ, and God put his stamp of ownership on you by giving you the Holy Spirit he had promised. [14]The Spirit is the guarantee that we shall receive what God has promised his people, and this assures us that God will give complete freedom to those who are his. Let us praise his glory! (GNT)**

That simply means that when you accepted Jesus, God put His *stamp of approval* on you by putting His Spirit in you. Along with His approval, He gives you a guarantee that you now belong to Him, and that He has an inheritance for you to partake of—in this life and the next one too.

This is wonderful news! However, this does bring up a question: Can we keep living sinful lives after we get saved?

Absolutely not! The Bible answers that question in Romans 6:1–2.

> **Shall we continue in sin that grace may abound? ²Certainly not! How shall we who died to sin live any longer in it?** (NKJV)

You see, your old nature (your old self) is now dead. You are a new creation who is alive unto God. The old nature was a slave to sin, but now that your old self has died and you have been raised up as a new creature in Christ Jesus, you have been freed from sin. You are now dead to sin.

Acts 3:19 tells us when we make Jesus our Lord and Savior, "our sins are blotted out." That means they are erased. God does not remember them anymore!

Therefore, sin does not have control over you anymore. You and Jesus are now in control of your life! The more you yield to Him living in you, the more His life will flow through you.

Furthermore, when a person genuinely receives Jesus as their Lord and Savior, they do not *want* to live in sin any longer. They want to turn from their past ways and live a new way.

Romans 2:4 tells us, "the goodness of God leads you to repentance?"

In essence, the word "repentance" means a reversal or change of direction. In other words, it is a 180 degree change of direction. You were going one way, following the path of sin and the lusts of your flesh, but now you have *turned* and have begun to follow God and His ways.

I like a couple of other translations of Romans 2:4.

> **Don't you realize that it is God's kindness that is trying to lead you to him and change the way you think and act? (GW)**

Don't you see how wonderfully kind, tolerant, and patient God is with you? Does this mean nothing to you? Can't you see that His kindness is intended to turn you from your sin? (NLT)

It really boils down to this: When you start enjoying the life that God has for you, you do not want to turn back to your old ways of living.

God truly loves us and only wants the best for our lives. He is a good God! And there is one thing you can be assured of—He will *always* be good to you!

CHAPTER 4

God Is Good—All the Time

God is not good some days and bad other days. No! He is ALWAYS good. The Bible says that God never changes.

The Book of James tells us that only good and perfect things come down from our Father God in Heaven. It also says that He does not vary or change. That means He does not send good things into our lives one day, and then evil things the next.

This truth is clearly revealed in James 1:13–17. Let us take a look at it.

> Don't blame God when you are tempted! God cannot be tempted by evil, and he doesn't use evil to tempt others. [14]We are tempted by our own desires that drag us off and trap us. [15]Our desires make us sin, and when sin is finished with us, it

leaves us dead. [16]Don't be fooled, my dear friends. [17]Every good and perfect gift comes down from the Father who created all the lights in the heavens. He is always the same and never makes dark shadows by changing. (CEV)

God is not the one who is behind all the dark and evil things that are happening in the earth today. All of them originate from the kingdom of darkness ruled by Satan.

Many Christians do not have a grasp on this truth, so they blame God when evil things happen.

I encourage you to do a study in the Bible of the two words "good" and "evil." There is a big difference between the two.

Once you see what the Bible calls "good" and what it calls "evil" then you will know what comes from God and what does not. This will help you to know what you should accept as the will of God for your life, and what you should reject.

Isaiah 5:20 tells us not to be mixed up by saying something is good when it is evil. (If you would like to learn more about this subject, we offer an audio series on our website titled, "Did God Do This?")

In the tenth chapter of John's Gospel, Jesus calls Himself the "good Shepherd." He uses an analogy, likening Himself to a natural shepherd who takes care of a flock of sheep.

By placing the word "good" before the word shepherd, Jesus lets us know that He only does the *good* things that are associated with what a shepherd does when caring for his flock.

There are at least four things we can learn from this analogy.

1. A *good shepherd* never leaves his flock alone.

2. A *good shepherd* always guards and protects his flock from wolves and all other enemies.

3. A *good shepherd* always leads his sheep to places where they are well fed.

4. A *good shepherd* always tends to any sheep that need help, even carrying them in times of trouble.

Therefore—this is what Jesus will do for you:

1.   Jesus will never leave you alone.

He said in Matthew 28:20, "I am with you always, even until the end of the world."

You never have to pray and ask God to go with you. He has taken up residence inside of you, therefore—He goes everywhere you go!

2. Jesus will always guard you and protect you.

Psalm 84:11

> **The LORD is our protector and glorious king, blessing us with kindness and honor. He does not refuse any good thing to those who do what is right.** (GNT)

Proverbs 30:5

> Every word of God proves true. He is a shield to all who come to Him for protection. (NLT)

Psalm 18:2

> The LORD is my protector; he is my strong fortress. My God is my protection, and with him I am safe. He protects me like a shield; he defends me and keeps me safe. (GNT)

3. Jesus will always lead you along the right paths, and will always provide for you in abundance.

John 10:10

> I came that you may have and enjoy life, and have it in abundance (to the full, till it overflows). (AMPC)

Psalm 16:11

> You will show me the path of life. In Your presence is fullness of joy. At

your right hand there are pleasures for evermore. (NKJV)

Psalm 32:8

I will guide you along the best pathway for your life. I will advise you and watch over you. (NLT)

Psalm 34:10

…they that seek the Lord shall not want any good thing.

4. Jesus will always be there for you, helping you through the good times and the challenging ones.

Isaiah 46:4

I will be your God throughout your lifetime—until your hair is white with age. (NLT)

Hebrews 4:16

Let us therefore come boldly unto the throne of grace, that we may obtain mercy, and find grace to help in time of need.

Matthew 11:28–29

> Come to me, all you who are troubled and weighted down with care, and I will give you rest. [29]Take my yoke on you and become like me, for I am gentle and without pride, and you will have rest for your souls. (BBE)

One of my favorite Bible passages is found in Isaiah. It has helped me many times through the years as I have faced the tests and trials of life.

Look at Isaiah 40:28–31.

> Have you not known? Have you not heard, that God is timeless and limitless, that He is the LORD, the One who made everything on planet earth, and that He does not faint or grow tired? He already has everything figured out. [29]He gives power to those who are exhausted; and to them who feel powerless He gives them His strength. [30]Even teenagers will get tired and

become exhausted, and young men will become weak and fall down: [31]But those who join themselves to the LORD shall exchange their strength for His; they will arise to new heights just like the eagles; they will run right through their obstacles without fatigue; and they will move forward as leaders and not burn out. (My Paraphrase)

Jesus is definitely a GOOD SHEPHERD! You can call on him at any time, for anything—in the bad times and the good!

If you want your Bible doctrine to always be correct, remember this:

GOOD GOD—BAD DEVIL

CHAPTER 5

Another Gift

In chapter three we discovered that salvation is a gift, given by God's grace, and received by believing (faith).

Everything you receive from God is received by faith. And what you believe (your faith) must always be based on what Jesus has already done for you.

That being said, there is another gift that God wants you to receive. It is talked about in the Book of Acts.

In the Second Chapter of Acts, there were one hundred and twenty believers gathered together seeking God. Look at what Verse 4 says:

> **And they were all** *filled with the Holy Spirit* **and began to speak with**

**other tongues, as the Spirit gave
them utterance.**

It says they were all *filled with the Holy
Spirit*. In Verse 38, Peter calls it the *gift of the
Holy Spirit*. Then, in Verse 39, he says this
gift was not only available for those to whom
he was speaking, but for all of us in future
generations as well.

Look at the fourth verse again:

**And they were all filled with the
Holy Spirit and** *began to speak with
other tongues,* **as the Spirit gave
them utterance.**

God gave them a new language! He
gave them the ability to speak in a Heavenly
language.

This did not just happen in Acts 2. We see
more believers being filled with the Holy Spirit
and speaking in tongues in Acts 10:44–46, Acts
11:15–17, and Acts 19:1–6.

WHAT IS THE PURPOSE?

Speaking in a Heavenly tongue is vital for every believer today. Let us read some Scriptures and discover why.

In 1st Corinthians 14:2, the Apostle Paul writes, "For he who speaks in a [Heavenly] tongue does not speak to men but to God, for no one understands him; however, in the spirit he speaks mysteries" (NKJV—My emphasis added in brackets).

There are four very important things I want you to see in this verse.

First of all, it says, "For he who speaks in a [Heavenly] tongue *does not speak to men but to God...*"

When a believer speaks in this Heavenly language, they are not speaking to people, they are speaking to God. That means they are not speaking to themselves either. Speaking in tongues is a direct line to Heaven!

Next, the verse says, "...for *no one understands him.*"

That means the human mind cannot comprehend what is being said. In Verse 14, Paul says that when he prayed in tongues, his brain did not have a clue what he was saying!

Next, verse 2 says, "...*in the Spirit he speaks...*"

That means you are not talking out of your head, you are talking directly out of your spirit—and you have the Holy Spirit helping you.

The next thing verse 2 says is, "...*he speaks mysteries.*"

The word "mysteries " also means secrets. Speaking in tongues is a way to talk secrets with God!

When a believer speaks (prays) in tongues, he is praying out the perfect will of God for his life and the lives of others.

The devil hates when we believers pray in the spirit because he does not know what we are talking to God about. The things we are saying are divine secrets. He lost all divinity when he was booted out of heaven, so he cannot get in on the conversation.

That is why he fights so hard to convince Christians that speaking in an unknown tongue is "of the devil." He knows if he can get Christians to believe that, then they will not receive this free gift which empowers them to live supernaturally.

In Acts 1:8 Jesus said you receive power from Heaven when you receive this gift.

Therefore, when you pray in tongues, you are releasing a power that will alter the course of people's lives—including yours!

Paul went on in 1st Corinthians 14:4 saying, "He that speaks in a [Heavenly] tongue *edifies himself*..."

This verse reveals yet another benefit of praying in the spirit (in tongues).

Paul said you "edify" yourself. This word means to build up and to embolden. When you pray in the spirit, you strengthen yourself in the Lord, and build up your boldness as a witness for Him.

Paul adds two more benefits in verses 16 and 17. Verse 16 says we can bless the Lord in tongues, and verse 17 shows us it is an excellent way to give thanks to God.

This means that we can not only bless the Lord and give Him thanks in our own way, with our own limited understanding, but we can also bless Him and give Him thanks in a perfect and limitless way too (in tongues). So cool!

The Apostle Jude had something to say about the benefits of praying in the Spirit as well.

Jude 1:20–21

> **Beloved, build up yourselves on your most holy faith, praying in the Holy Spirit. [21]Keeping yourselves in the love of God, looking for the mercy of our Lord Jesus Christ unto eternal life.**

Jude reiterates what Paul said about building up ourselves, but adds that it helps our faith to stay strong. Then, he says it helps to keep us operating in the love of God.

If you want your faith to work, God's grace to flow, and to live the abundant life God has for you, you must abide in His love. Therefore, we definitely want to pray in tongues often. Which is why the Apostle Paul said, "I pray in tongues more than all of you" (1st Corinthians 14:18).

How to Receive the Gift

Once a believer sees the benefits of being filled with the Holy Spirit, they always want to receive this free gift from God.

By now, you may be thinking, "How do I receive this gift?"

The answer is: You ask! I know, that sounds simple right? But is that not how you got saved in the first place?

Look at Luke 11:9–13.

Listen, it is as simple as this: Ask and it will be given to you. Seek and you will find. Knock and the door will be opened. [10]For everyone who asks shall receive, and everyone who seeks shall find, and everyone who knocks will have a door opened. [11]If a son asks his father for a piece of bread, will the father give him a stone? What if the son asks for a piece of fish, will the father give him a snake instead? [12]Or what if the son asks for an egg, will the father offer him a scorpion? [13]Of course he wouldn't! Even a sinful father knows how to give good gifts to his children. So, you can be absolutely assured that your Heavenly Father will do much more than an earthly father. If you ask Him for the Holy Spirit, the gift is yours! (My Paraphrase)

Wow! God has made it so simple. The same way you received Jesus as your Lord and Savior, is the same way you receive the gift of the Holy Spirit. You ask and believe you receive Him.

Once you receive Him, you have the ability to speak in a brand new Heavenly prayer language.

Go for it! And feel free to call us if you need any more help. We are here for you!

CHAPTER 6

Your Lifeline

One of the most important things a Christian can do, is to learn what God has to say in the Bible. There are two ways to learn God's Word. 1. By reading your Bible. 2. By hearing the Word of God taught. Both must be on a regular and consistent basis.

First of all, get a Bible and read it. It contains God's thoughts and His ways. Isaiah 58:7–11, tells us how important it is to follow God and His ways, not the ways of the ungodly. It also says that God's Word contains His thoughts and ways, and when we plant them on the inside of us, they will produce a harvest. That means His thoughts and His ways become ours.

In John 6:63 Jesus said, "The words that I speak to you are spirit and life."

God's Words are containers of "spirit" and "life."

"Spirit" refers to supernatural and eternal things. "Life" refers to the Life that comes from God Himself.

That is why I stated above that the Word of God is your LIFE LINE.

In Matthew 4:4 Jesus said, "Humans are not supposed to live just by eating natural food. They should also be living supernaturally, by consuming God's food for their spirit-man. That food only comes from the words out of the mouth of God" (My Paraphrase).

When you were born-again, God made you a new person on the inside. But He did not change your body or your mind (intellect).

The real you is an eternal, supernatural being (a spirit). However, you are living inside a natural, temporal body, and possess a natural mind. Your mind has the capacity to learn God's thoughts and His ways. Now it is up to you to feed upon God's Word so that your mind gets renewed, or reprogrammed, to think properly.

Look at Romans 12:1–2. In Verse One, God tells us to keep our bodies pure, to live morally blameless, and to live in a way that is fully agreeable with the God-kind of lifestyle. It is part of our divine service to God.

In Verse Two He says, "Do not conform your life to the lifestyles of the ungodly. *Reprogram your thinking*, so that you can discern and choose to follow the will of God for your life. For it will cause things to go well in your life, make you fully agreeable and well-pleasing to God, and will help complete your character, both morally and mentally" (My Paraphrase).

"Reprogram your thinking." You do that by reading, speaking, and meditating on God's Word. When you do, Joshua 1:8 says "...then you will make your way prosperous, and you will have good success."

Jesus wants you prosperous and successful in every area of your life!

So, make sure you spend time in God's Word every day. You do not even have to have a Bible in your hand to do that. You can write down a verse on a piece of paper, stick it in your pocket, and use it throughout the day. Doing so will feed your spirit and release His life into your midst.

Next, find a church that believes Jesus is still the same today as when He walked the earth. He is still a savior, healer, miracle worker, Holy Ghost baptizer, deliverer, and LORD.

He still wants to do only good things for His family (you and me).

Hebrew 10:25 says, "Do not stop gathering together as Christians the way some have done. Get together and pray together. It is more important now than ever, especially since the return of Jesus is drawing near" (My Paraphrase).

It is vital to your spiritual growth that you become part of a church family. But, make sure you find one that believes in the complete salvation package (i.e., God wants you prosperous, free, healthy, and whole in every area of your life) spiritually, mentally, physically, financially, and socially.

Once you find the church that you feel in your heart God wants you to attend, plant yourself there. Psalm 92:13 says you will flourish and grow when you are planted in a good church.

The local church is a family of believers. Once you become part of a church family you will have people that will love you, help you, protect you, guide you, and strengthen you. It will help you learn to live a better life and walk closer to God.

Also, your Pastor will help you discover your gifts and callings, so that God can use you to be a blessing to others.

If you need our help in locating a good Bible-believing church, give us a call or email us and we will be happy to help you.

Thirdly, listen to good Ministers regularly on TV, radio, podcasts, the internet, and other forms of audio media. Our website offers a lot of materials that you can use to feed on the Word of God as well.

If you would like a list of other Ministers that we can recommend for you to learn from, send us an email and we will help you out.

CHAPTER 7

Talking with God

Having a conversation with God is not hard. It is not putting on some kind of religious voice and then trying to sound holy.

Have you ever been driving down the road with your spouse, or a friend, and just talked to them about some things that were on your mind? That is how you carry on a conversation with God. In truth, that is what the Bible calls "prayer."

Remember this: When God "saved" you, He placed Himself inside you by putting the Holy Spirit in you. He is with you all the time, everywhere you go. So just talk to Him in your normal voice. In fact, talk to God about everything.

First Peter 3:12 says, "For the eyes of the Lord are over the righteous, and his ears are open unto their prayers."

Since you are now "righteous", God is watching over you. But He is also hearing what you say to Him and listening to your questions—with an eagerness to answer them!

He said in Jeremiah 33:3, "Call upon me and I will answer you, and reveal things to you that nobody else knows but me" (My Paraphrase).

Therefore, talk to Him about everything.

God Talks Too

The Bible shows us numerous ways that God can speak to an individual.

In the Old Testament we see Him speak in an audible voice, through a donkey, through a burning bush, through Prophets, and through dreams and visions. He is God after all, so He can use whatever vessel He wants!

In the New Testament, we see Him speak through dreams, visions, Apostles, Prophets, Evangelists, Pastors, Teachers, angels, and other believers. On occasion, Jesus Himself even appeared to people and talked with them.

However, the *main way* that God speaks to all of His children today, is by His Spirit that lives on the inside of each one of them.

When the Holy Spirit communicates to us we usually do not hear a voice with our ears. Although there may be times when He speaks very authoritatively, and the person feels like he heard it audibly. That is because it was so clear, just as if a normal person was talking to him.

I have heard many Christians testify that they have heard a strong voice say, "Pull off the road now!" They did, and it spared their lives from being in an accident a few minutes later.

When He speaks to us like that, it is just as if a person said it, even though we do not actually hear it with our ears.

Another way the Holy Spirit speaks to us is by what the Bible calls "a still, small voice."

When the Holy Spirit speaks to His children in this manner, it is referred to by many as "a hunch" or, "a knowing."

This is one of the primary ways the Holy Spirit leads us.

In John 16:13, when Jesus was talking about the Holy Spirit coming to live inside man, he said, "...after He has come, He will guide you into all *truth*..."

That is an important statement, because the Holy Spirit *always* guides us and speaks to us with "truth" which is the Word of God.

The Holy Spirit will never tell you anything that is contradictory to the Bible.

Jesus continues in the above verse saying, "The Holy Spirit will not talk about Himself, *but will always speak of me*..."

If you will get that ingrained inside of you, it will keep you from a lot of troubles.

The Word of God (the Bible), is the manual that our Teacher, The Holy Spirit, uses to teach us—PERIOD! It is the *only thing* He uses! He never uses evil, misfortunes, accidents, illnesses, or destructive acts of nature to teach us.

If those things occur in our lives, and we will listen to Him while we are going through them, He will definitely show us how to escape them. He will also teach us how to avoid them in the future.

1st Corinthians 10:13

> **No one is exempt from tests and trials. We all will have them come our way. But when they do, we can be assured of God's faithfulness. He will be right there with us to see us through, He won't allow it to be more than what we can handle, and He will even show us the best way out.** (Author's Paraphrase)

Remember James 1:13–17 that we looked at earlier—God never uses any kind of evil in His dealings with us!

So, again, The Holy Spirit leads us and guides us by speaking the Word of God to us.

In John 14:26 Jesus again speaking of The Holy Spirit says, "He will teach you all things, He will remind you of things, and He is only going to say what I say" (Author's Paraphrase).

Different Means

When The Holy Spirit is speaking to us and teaching us, He does it through various means.

1. Your Pastor

This is very important!

The Holy Spirit uses Pastors to teach us. Jeremiah 3:15 tells us that God will use Pastors to feed us knowledge and understanding. Therefore, find a good Word-based church, and be faithful to attend when they have services.

2. Other Ministers

Listen to Ministers on TV and other forms of media. Whether it is TV, websites, Facebook, Twitter, blogs, books, or audio recordings, there are a lot of good preachers you can learn from. If you will use the things you have learned in this book as a guideline, you will know which ones to listen to and which ones you should not listen to.

Another way the Holy Spirit talks to us and leads us is by "peace."

For example, we may talk to God about a situation where we need some guidance. So, we ask the Lord, "Lord, should I do such-and-such?" While we are waiting to hear something, we actually have "a good feeling on the inside" about doing it.

That "peace" is one of the primary ways God directs us!

Isaiah 55:8–12 tells us that when we learn God's thoughts and ways, by learning His Word, then we will "go out with joy, and *be led by peace.*"

Notice, God will lead you by His *peace* on the inside of you. He often communicates to us in that way.

Romans 14:19 tells us to "follow after peace." Colossians 3:15 tells us to use "peace" as our umpire in life—allowing it to rule us and be our guide.

So, when you talk to God about decisions that you need to make, and you do not hear anything specifically, then go ahead and move forward. If you continually have peace as you go, then God is giving you His okay.

However, if you do not have peace, then stop! You do not want to do something without God's blessings. That is when we get ourselves into all kinds of messes.

You have probably heard about someone who got into a mess, and then heard them say, "I knew I wasn't supposed to do that" or, "Something told me I wasn't supposed to..."

Do not take lightly that still, small voice. It will lead you out of trouble, and into the blessings of heaven!

CHAPTER 8

The Best Financial Advisor Ever!

If you were to sit down with a Financial Advisor, what would be the purpose of his counsel?

The most simplistic answer to that question would be, "To help me improve my financial status."

True. Whether it is to stop spending more than you earn, pay off debt, put away savings, or tell you about investment opportunities, they would attempt to give you financial counsel that would help your financial status in the future.

Well...guess who has more wisdom in that area than any man alive? Yep, you guessed it—your Father God!

Think about it: God created the earth and everything in it. He created the gold, the silver, the oil, the gas, every precious stone, the herbs, fish and meats that we eat, and every other valuable item you can name.

Who did He create it all for? You and me! That is right, Genesis, Chapters One and Two show us He made it all for us.

Psalm 115:16 tells us the same thing—He made it all for us!

Since God is the creator of all the wealth in the earth, does it not stand to reason that He knows more about it than any human being? Of course He does!

Psalm 104:24 says, "O LORD, how numerous are your works! You have used your wisdom to make all of earth's possessions. The earth is overflowing with all the creatures and wealth that you created" (My Paraphrase).

Since God used His wisdom to make all the riches in the earth, then obviously He has more wisdom on the subject than any man.

If we want to have an abundance of wealth on this earth, and use it properly, then we must learn from its Maker.

In October of 1908, the first Model-T Ford automobile was produced. Guess who showed people how to use it? The maker—Henry Ford.

In 1976, the first Apple computer was made. Guess who showed people how to use it? The developer—Steve Wozniak.

God, being the Maker and Developer of the earth and its abundant resources, has a system set up whereby His children can partake of and enjoy using the wealth and riches that are here.

Learning and using God's wisdom regarding this subject will protect us from greed, covetousness, and the deceitfulness of riches.

Proverbs 23:4 says, "Labor not to be rich: cease from your own wisdom."

Proverbs 2:6 says, "For the LORD gives wisdom: out of his mouth comes knowledge and understanding."

So, let us learn some things that God has to say about our financial prosperity and how to handle it.

FIRST THINGS FIRST

In Matthew 6:24, Jesus tells us that He is supposed to be our Master, not money. We are supposed to serve God and let money serve us.

He goes on in verses 25–32 telling us that we do not have to worry about acquiring the necessities of life. God wants to provide those things for us.

Then He says in verse 33, "Seek first the kingdom of God and His righteousness and all these things shall be added to you."

My paraphrase of that verse is: "Make sure your top priority in life is to do things the way God tells you to do them. He has made you righteous, so live right. Then you can be assured that He will increase you financially, and you will have need of nothing."

Since we want God in charge of our financial prosperity, we must put Him first in that area, just like we do in every other area of our lives. When you put God first in your money matters, He will bring abundant provision to you financially.

In Genesis 14, Abraham went to battle and defeated some wicked kings. He fought them to retrieve his nephew and others who had been kidnapped, as well as a huge amount of stolen riches. Not only did Abraham get everything back, but he also took all the wealth of the kings whom he had defeated.

Upon returning from the battle he met with Melchizedek, who was God's representative, and gave him "tithes" of all his increase (Genesis 14:20).

The word "tithes" means ten percent. That means Abraham took the first dime out of every dollar and gave it to God.

THAT IS VERY IMPORTANT! Because in the very first verse of the next chapter, God says to Abraham, "Because you have made me Lord of your money, you don't have to worry about anything. I'm going to protect you, and I'm going to be your source for abundant financial provision" (Genesis 15:1, My paraphrase).

When Abraham tithed in Genesis 14, there was not a commandment to do so. He was not under any law, and did not have to put God first—but he did!

Abraham, like us in the New Testament, was under grace. He "believed" God and it was "accounted to him" for righteousness. His faith received God's grace.

To Abraham, tithing was not a law issue, but a Lordship issue. He did not *have* to do it, he *wanted* to.

When we obey God because we *want* to, our will is involved. That is when it becomes a heart issue, and a faith issue that pleases God.

When you study out tithing in the Bible, you will see that tithing started long before there was any law that made you do it. It was later incorporated into the Law of Moses (as a commandment) in the Old Testament, and then it was continued in the New Testament.

When we tithe, we are putting God first in our finances and declaring Him as LORD of our money. That puts Him in control of our financial affairs.

God has a million-and-one-ways to prosper us that we have not even thought of yet, so we should want Him in charge. Besides that, it brings Him great pleasure to prosper us!

Look at Psalm 35:27.

> **Let them shout for joy and be glad, Who favor my righteous cause; And let them say continually, Let the LORD be magnified, Who has pleasure in the prosperity of His servant.**

So, whether you are already financially free, or just struggling to make ends meet, begin tithing today and God will increase you more and more.

You will also find that the Bible teaches the giving of offerings. Tithing is giving the first ten percent of all monies that come to you. Offerings are any thing you give above the tithe. As you will soon learn, the more you give to God, the more harvest He will return to you.

I will conclude this subject with this: God did not create wealth for us to love, covet, or use wrongfully. He created it for us to enjoy, and to share with others.

First Timothy 6:17–18 says this:

> **Give this message to those who are abounding with wealth: Never allow yourself to think or act like you are better than someone else because of what you have. And do not ever yield to the temptation that money and things will make you happy—they are unreliable! You keep your trust and confidence fixed upon God, who is your life. He will not only give you an abundace of riches, but He wants you to enjoy having them. [18]In addition, do good**

things with your wealth—always ready to pass on the blessings to others, and be willing and liberal when you do.(My Paraphrase)

CHAPTER 9

Health for the Physical Body

Earlier we discovered that salvation is a gift, given by God's grace, and received through faith (Ephesians 2:8).

The words "saved" and "salvation" come from the Greek word *sozo*. It means: saved, preserved, protected, healed, made whole.

Notice, part of your salvation package includes health and wholeness for your physical body.

When Jesus was on the cross bearing your sins, He also bare your sicknesses and diseases—so that you do not have to (See Isaiah 53:4 and Matthew 8:17).

First Peter 2:24 declares "...by His stripes (blow, bruise) you were healed." That is not talking about spiritual healing. You were not *healed* spiritually, you were *recreated* spiritually.

So this verse is referring to healing for your physical body.

When God laid on Jesus your sins, He also laid on Him every other curse known to mankind, which included all your sicknesses and diseases.

Here is the Good News: It is just as easy to receive your healing as it was to receive your forgiveness of sin. You do it the same way. By grace (God's favor) are you saved (healed) through faith (believing).

You receive your healing by faith the same way your received your forgiveness by faith. Since healing and forgiveness are part of the salvation package, then they are both available to everyone!

If you ever hear someone say, "It is not God's will to heal everybody," just remember— SALVATION IS FOR EVERYBODY, AND HEALING IS PART OF SALVATION.

We encourage you to read through the four Gospels, and take note when any sick person came to Jesus for healing. He healed them all. And the Bible declares that Jesus is the same today as when He physically walked the earth (Hebrews 13:8).

He healed everyone who would believe back then, and He will still heal everyone who will believe today!

Mark 9:23 "All things are possible to him who believes."

CHAPTER 10

Authority and Dominion

God has a bright future planned out for you. He wants you to live a life filled with abundance.

But you need to be aware that there is an enemy arrayed against you who wants to bring harm and destruction your way.

You see, before you were born into the Kingdom of God you were part of the kingdom of darkness (by default).

Those who are not saved are part of the kingdom of darkness, even though they do not know it. The kingdom of darkness is ruled by Satan, also known as the Devil.

He is not one for us to fear, as he has no power over a child of God! When Jesus rose from the dead He totally stripped Satan of all his power to harm a child of God.

First John 3:8 says, "...For this purpose the Son of God was manifested, that he might destroy the works of the devil."

A study of Scripture reveals the works of the devil are: sin, sickness, pain (both emotional and physical), poverty, and all types of evil in the world.

We can easily see those "works" are still running rampant in the earth today. So, what does it mean that Jesus came to "destroy" the works of the devil?

The word "destroy" means to loosen. That means Jesus "loosened" us from, or set us free from, the works of Satan.

The only way the devil can put any of his works on a child of God is by deception. Revelation 12:9 calls him a deceiver. That is why God warns us to be on our guard.

Look at 1st Peter 5:8.

Stay alert! Watch out for your great enemy, the devil. He prowls around

like a roaring lion, looking for someone to devour. (NLT)

Then Verse 9 tells us to use our faith to stop him. That means we can!

Ephesians 6:16 says, "Let your faith be like a shield, and you will be able to stop all the flaming arrows of the evil one" (CEV).

When we put our faith in The Word of God, believing in what Jesus has done for us, our faith becomes an impenetrable shield that will stop all of Satan's attacks.

Furthermore, you have dominion and authority over the devil and his works. Look at what Jesus told us in Matthew 28:18–19.

All authority is given to me in heaven and in earth. [19]You go therefore and teach all people... (NKJV)

When Jesus said "you go therefore" He delegated His authority to us.

In Luke 9:1–2 Jesus gave His disciples power and authority over all devils and all diseases. He did the same thing for seventy other believers (like you and me) in Luke 10. Then He spoke to *every believer* in John 14:12, when He said, "Everyone who believes in me will be able to do everything they see me doing" (My Paraphrase).

Luke 10:19 reveals that Jesus has given us authority over all the power of the devil so that he cannot harm us. However, we must use our authority. James 4:7 tells us to submit to God, then resist the devil—and he has to obey us!

We do not have to be afraid of anyone or anything. I strongly encourage you to study the verses in the Bible that say "fear not" or any form of that, i.e. do not fear, do not be afraid, etc.

That study will help you stay free from all forms of fear, including panic attacks, anxiety, stress, worry, and much more!

CONCLUSION

You have exciting days ahead of you as you learn to walk with the Lord Jesus on a daily basis.

One thing I wish I had done when I had just been saved was to study the Scriptures that talk about *who God says I am, what God says belongs to me,* and *what He says that I can do* as a child of the most high God.

It was many years after I was saved that I learned about these things—and it was LIFE TRANSFORMING!

These three things are vital if you want to live an abundant life. If you do not already have our series entitled "He Was, I Am" then I would strongly encourage you to obtain it, as it is over five hours of teaching on these three things.

Also, you will want to buy a Bible that is easy to read and understand, the New Living Translation is a good one.

JESUS CAME IN MY ROOM

Years ago the Lord came to me and said, "I'm going to show you how to never have another down day for the rest of your life." He went on to expound that He meant having total control over my feelings, such as anger, depression, stress, worry, fear, discouragement, grief, hurt feelings, guilt, or shame. He said that if I would do what He showed me, then none of those negative emotions would control me ever again. He said I would have complete control over my feelings and emotions.

Well, He showed me exactly what to do, and guess what? I haven't had a down day since! Now that Jesus showed me what to do, I don't allow bad temper, stress, fear, depression or any other negative emotion to control me anymore. I control how I feel—not other people or situations!

THIS IS VITALLY IMPORTANT, as our emotions play a huge part in every area of our lives. Negative emotions have destroyed marriages, brought on many physical illnesses, caused financial problems, and made life miserable for far too many Christians. But Jesus made a way for all of His children to be free mentally and emotionally too!

The reason I didn't cover this topic in this book is because it would take up the whole book. In fact, I have an audio series entitled *Free From Me* and a book entitled *Internal Affairs: Emotional Stability in an Unstable World*. These materials will show you exactly what Jesus taught me, and how you can live in peace and joy, 24 hours a day—365 days a year!

You can order or download these materials from our website, www.larryhutton.org.

ONE LAST THING

Proverbs 18:21 tells us what happens when we speak words out of our mouth. It says we either release "life" or "death" into our lives. *Life* refers to things like right living, health, prosperity, peace, joy, and success, whereas, death refers to wrong living, sickness, poverty, stress, depression and failure.

Our words shape our future, so it is vitally important to speak blessings into our lives. The only way we are going to speak "life" is when we speak God's Word.

So, we have made it easy for you, by producing what I call "Declare It" cards. They are 52 cards in an attractive acrylic box about the size of a deck of cards with a scripture on one side, and my personal confession on the other. Take one with you every day and learn to speak life and release God's life into yours.

Hey Friend, if we can assist you in finding a good church, direct you to any specific teaching materials, or help you in any other way with your Christian walk, please let us know. You can order materials, or contact us through our website at www.larryhutton.org, or call us M–F, 9am–5pm at (918) 259-3077.

Fast. Easy. Convenient.

For the latest Harrison House product information and author news, look no further than your computer. All the details on our powerful, life-changing products are just a click away. New releases, email subscriptions, testimonies, monthly specials—find them all in one place.

harrisonhouse.com